SECOND EDITION
Super Practice Book

# 1

SUPER PRACTICE

Emma Szlachta · Garan Holcombe

CAMBRIDGE
UNIVERSITY PRESS

# Map of the Book

| Unit | Grammar/Language | Reading/Writing | Listening/Speaking |
|---|---|---|---|
| (pages 4–11) | • Numbers<br>• Colors | A Chat | Greetings |
| 1 (pages 12–19) | • Questions and Short Answers<br>• Imperatives | A Comic Strip | Classroom Objects |
| 2 (pages 20–27) | • *What's his/her ... ?*<br>*How old is he/she?*<br>• Adjectives | An Email | Toys and Friends |
| 3 (pages 28–35) | • *In, On, Under*<br>• *I like / I don't like ...* | A Project | Animals |
| 4 (pages 36–43) | • *I have / I don't have ...*<br>• *Do ... have any ... ?* | A Text Message | Food |
| 5 (pages 44–51) | • Free-Time Activities<br>• *Do you ... ? Yes, I do. / No, I don't.* | A Blog | Free-Time Activities |
| 6 (pages 52–59) | • *There's / There are ...*<br>• *Is there / Are there ... ?*<br>*How many ... ?* | A Project | Houses and Rooms |
| 7 (pages 60–67) | • *Do you like this/these ... ?*<br>• *Is he/she + -ing?* | A Chat | Clothes |
| 8 (pages 68–75) | • *Can/Can't* for Ability<br>• Questions with *Can* | A Forum | The Body and Actions |
| 9 (pages 76–83) | • Suggestions<br>• *Where's / Where are ... ?* | A Magazine | Vacations |

# Numbers

## Language Focus

Use **How old are you?** and **I'm ...** to ask and answer about ages.

**How old are you?**   **I'm** *nine.*
                       **I'm** *ten.*

## 1  Match the numbers.

How old are you?

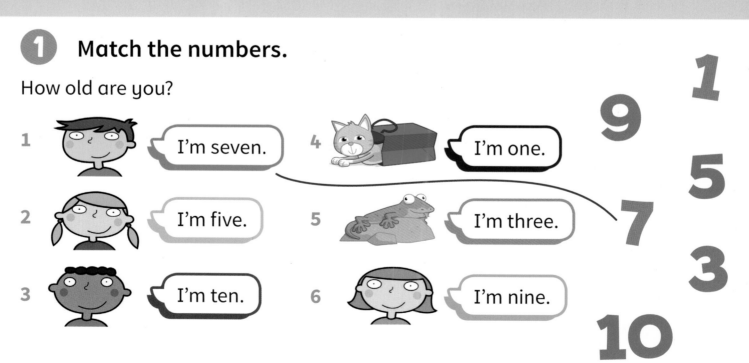

**2** Follow the numbers in the maze.

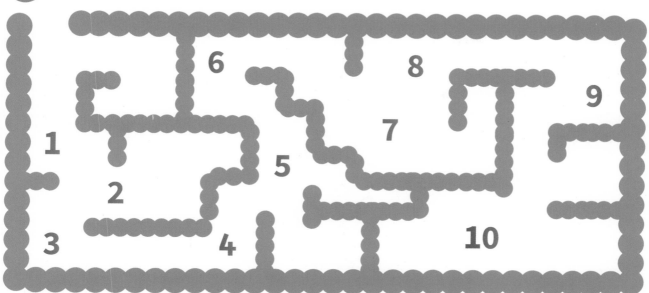

1   2   3   4   5   6   7   8   9   10

**3** Write the numbers.

1

one

2

3

4

5

6

7

8

9

10

# Colors

I'm Ned. My hat is blue.

I'm Ben. My hat is green.

What's your name?

**Language Focus**

Use **colors** to describe different objects.
*A **blue** hat.     My hat is **green**.*

**1**   Match the colors with the words.

1 blue

2 orange

3 yellow

4 red

5 green

6 purple

## 2 Write the letters to complete the colors.

1 gr __e__ __e__ n

2 o ___ a ___ ___ e

3 r ___ ___

4 ___ ur ___ l ___

5 ___ e ___ l ___ w

6 b ___ ___ e

## 3 Write the colors.

1 A _____blue_____ balloon

2 A _____ balloon

3 A _____ balloon

4 A _____ balloon

5 A _____ balloon

6 An _____ balloon

# Reading: A Chat

**1** Read the conversation and match the phrases.

**Sally Green**

Hi! I'm Sally. What's your name?

**Hugo Black**

I'm Hugo. How old are you?

**Sally Green**

I'm eight. How old are you?

**Hugo Black**

I'm seven.

| | |
|---|---|
| 1 Sally | a seven |
| 2 Hugo | b Green |
| 3 Sally is | c eight |
| 4 Hugo is | d Black |

**1** **Write the questions.**

1  you / old / How / are / ?

_____

2  your / name / What's / ?

_____

**2** **Write a conversation with a friend. Draw pictures.**

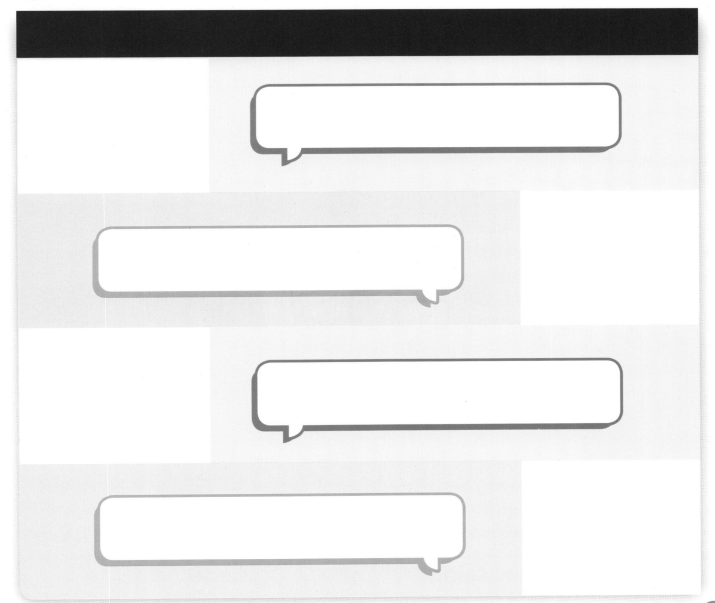

# Listening: Greetings

**1** 🎧 01 Listen and draw lines.

6  7  8  9

**2** 🎧 02 Listen and color.

**1** **Draw a picture of you with a hat and a balloon.**

**2** **Look at your picture and write answers. Then practice.**

1 What's your name?          I'm _____.

2 How old are you?          I'm _____.

3 What color is your hat?          My hat is _____.

4 What color is your balloon?          My balloon is _____.

**3** **Work with a friend. Ask and answer.**

Hi! I'm Tom. What color is your hat?

Hello! I'm Lucy. My hat is orange.

**Language Focus**

Use **What's this?** to ask about objects and **It's a ...** to answer.
Use **Is it ... ?** to ask about objects and **No, it isn't / Yes, it is** to give short answers.

***What's this?*** ***It's a*** pencil.   ***Is it*** a pen? ***No, it isn't.*** / ***Yes, it is.***

**1** **Look at the pictures. Match the questions with the responses.**

1 Is it an eraser?

2 Is it a pencil?

3 Is it a desk?

4 Is it a pencil case?

5 Is it a ruler?

6 Is it a bag?

Yes, it is.

No, it isn't.

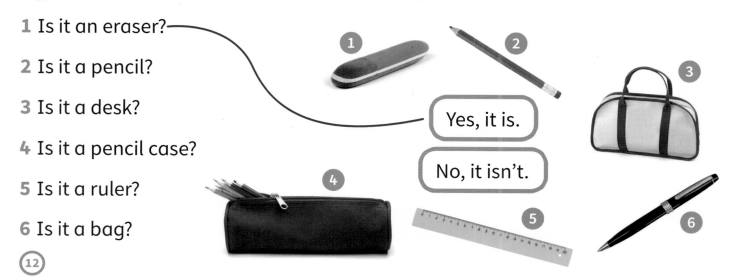

## 2 Match the questions with the responses.

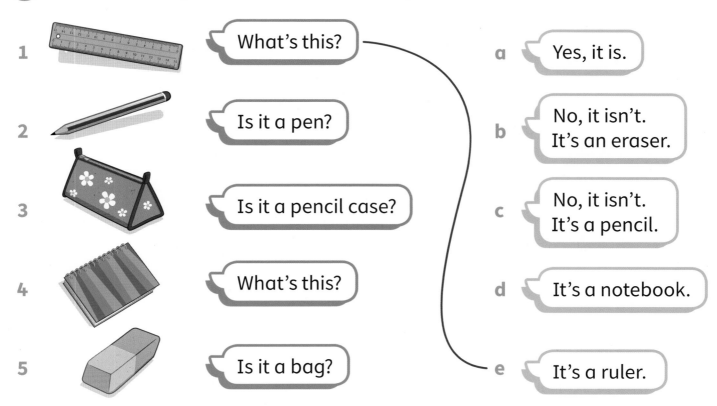

1. What's this?
2. Is it a pen?
3. Is it a pencil case?
4. What's this?
5. Is it a bag?

a. Yes, it is.
b. No, it isn't. It's an eraser.
c. No, it isn't. It's a pencil.
d. It's a notebook.
e. It's a ruler.

## 3 Write questions and answers.

1 this / What's / ?

__What's  this?__

a / It's / desk / .

_____

2 eraser / it / Is / an / ?

_____

is / Yes, / it / .

_____

3 it / notebook / Is / a / ?

_____

isn't / it / No, / .

_____

4 this / What's / ?

_____

a / It's / bag / green / .

_____

5 this / What's / ?

_____

a / desk / yellow / It's / .

_____

# Imperatives

Open your bag, please.

Put away your bag, please.

Sit at your desk, please.

Take out your pen, please.

**1** **Match the sentences with the pictures.**

1 Close your bag, please. **b**

2 Pass me a ruler, please. ☐

3 Take out your book, please. ☐

4 Pass me a pen, please. ☐

5 Take out your ruler, please. ☐

6 Open your bag, please. ☐

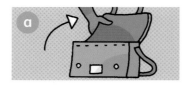

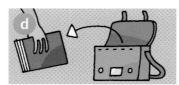

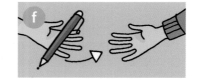

**2** **Complete the sentences with the words from the box.**

Put   Turn   Pass   Open   away   ~~Pass~~

1 **Pass** me a pencil, please.

2 _____ your books, please.

3 _____ around.

4 _____ your eraser on your head.

5 _____ me a ruler, please.

6 Put _____ your bags, please.

**3** **Look and write.**

1 Open **your bags** , please.

2 Sit at _____ .

3 Close _____ , please.

4 Pass _____ , please.

5 Take _____ please.

6 Put _____ , please.

# Reading: A Comic Strip

**1** Read the text and draw lines.

**1** What objects are on your desk and in your classroom?

a black book _____ _____ _____

_____ _____ _____ _____

**2** Write a story. Draw pictures.

# Listening: Classroom Objects

## 1 🎧 03 Listen and check ☑ the correct picture.

**1**
a ☑
b ☐

**2**
a ☐
b ☐

**3**
a ☐
b ☐

**4**
a ☐
b ☐ ENGLISH

**5**
a ☐
b ☐

**6**
a ☐
b ☐

## 2 🎧 04 Look at the box. Listen and do the actions.

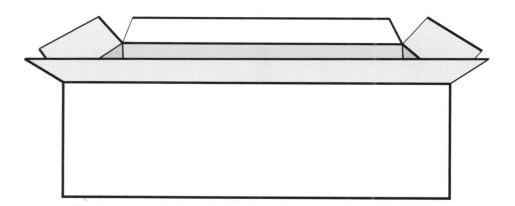

**1** **Look and write. Then ask and answer.**

> What's letter "a"?

> It's a pen.

a

b

c

d

___pen___ _____ _____ _____

**2** **Draw three classroom objects.**

**3** **Work with a friend. Talk about your classroom objects.**

> What's this?

> It's my pencil case. It's orange.

What's his name?

How old is he?

What's his favorite toy?

What's her name?

His name is Ben.

He's seven.

His favorite toy's his ball.

Her name is Grace. She's seven, and her favorite toy is a ball, too!

**Language Focus**

Asking and answering questions using **his**, **her**, **he**, and **she**.

| | |
|---|---|
| *What's **his** name?* | ***His** name's Ned.* |
| *How old is **he**?* | ***He**'s six.* |
| *What's **his** favorite toy?* | ***His** favorite toy's his ball.* |
| *What's **her** name?* | ***Her** name's Alice.* |
| *How old is **she**?* | ***She**'s eight.* |
| *What's **her** favorite toy?* | ***Her** favorite toy's her kite.* |

### 1  Match the questions with the responses.

1 What's her name?

2 What's her favorite toy?

3 How old is she?

4 What's his favorite toy?

5 What's his name?

6 How old is he?

a He's ten.

b His name's Tim.

c Her name's Kim.

d She's six.

e Her favorite toy's her bike.

f His favorite toy's his plane.

**2** **Complete the sentences with the words from the box.**

favorite   ~~her~~   She's   What's   name   she

1   What's __her__ name?          Her _____'s Sophie.

2   _____ her favorite toy?          Her _____ toy's her go-kart.

3   How old is _____?          _____ seven.

**3** **Write questions and answers.**

1 his / What's / name / ?          __What's his name?__

Ben / His / name's / .          _____

2 Toby / How / old / is / ?          _____

seven / He's / .          _____

3 his / What's / number / favorite / ?          _____

number / favorite / is / His / ten / .          _____

4 her / What's / name / ?          _____

name's / Mary / Her / .          _____

# Adjectives

It's a big yellow plane.

It's a long red train.

It's a new black go-kart.

It's an ugly orange monster!

## Language Focus

Use **an** before words beginning with **a**, **e**, **i**, **o**, or **u** (vowels).

It's *a new* kite.          It's *an ugly* monster.

It's *a long blue* train.          It's *a big green* ball.

**1** Look, read, and check ☑ or put an X ☒.

1 It's a long red train.          ☒
2 It's a big green ball.          ☐
3 It's an ugly purple monster.          ☐
4 It's a new pink go-kart.          ☐
5 It's a long blue train.          ☐
6 It's a big yellow ball.          ☐

**2** Circle the correct words to complete the sentences.

1 It's *a* / *an* short green train.

2 It's *a* / *an* ugly purple monster.

3 It's a *beautiful new* / *new beautiful* doll.

4 It's *a* / *an* small yellow ball.

5 It's a *green big* / *big green* monster.

6 It's *a* / *an* old black go-kart.

**3** Write sentences with *a/an* and the words from the box.

| ~~yellow bike~~   ugly green monster   yellow and red plane |
| beautiful doll   blue car   big ball |

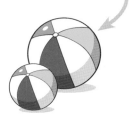

1 It's __a yellow bike__ .

2 It's _____.

3 It's _____.

4 It's _____.

5 It's _____.

6 It's_____.

# Reading: An Email

**1** Read the text and answer the questions.

To: Ana

From: Tom

Hi, Ana,

I'm Tom, and I'm seven. My favorite toy's my yellow go-kart. It's new! Look – this is my go-kart!

What's your favorite toy? How old are you?

Tom

To: Tom

From: Ana

Hi, Tom,

I'm seven. My favorite toy isn't a doll or a computer game. My favorite toy's my bike. It's a new green bike. My favorite color's green. Look – this is my bike! What's your favorite color?

Ana

1 What's his name?

His name's Tom.

2 How old is he?

3 What's his favorite toy?

4 What's her name?

5 What color is her bike?

6 What's her favorite color?

## 1 Write answers.

What's your favorite toy? _____

What color is it? _____

Is it new or old? _____

What isn't your favorite toy? _____

## 2 Write an email to Tom or Ana. Use your notes from Activity 1. Draw a picture of the toy.

To:

From:

**1** 🎧 **05** Listen and number the pictures.

a

b

c

1

d

**2** 🎧 **06** Listen and color.

**1** **Talk about the toys. Use the words.**

> Number 1 is a small pink monster.

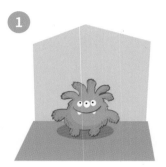

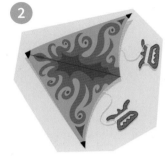

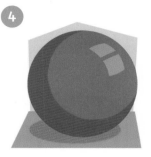

small pink

beautiful green

new orange

big red

**2** **Look at the toys in Activity 1. Play the guessing game.**

> It's new and orange. What is it?

> It's the go-kart.

**3** **Look at Activity 1 and choose a toy for a friend. Then write and say.**

My friend's name is _____ . He's/She's _____ .
This toy is for my friend. It's a _____ .

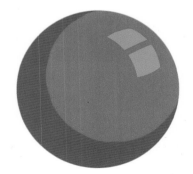

> My friend's name is Luc. He's six. This toy is for my friend. It's a big red ball.

# 3 In, On, Under

The dog is under the desk.     The cat is on the desk.     The rat is in the bag.

**Language Focus**

Use **prepositions** to describe where things are.

|  | *in* |  |
|---|---|---|
| *The lizard is* | ***on*** | *the bag.* |
|  | ***under*** |  |

**1** **Match the sentences with the pictures.**

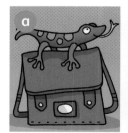

1 The cat is under the desk.  **b**

2 The frog is in the bag.  ☐

3 The lizard is on the bag.  ☐

4 The lizard is in the pencil case.  ☐

5 The rat is under the desk.  ☐

## 2  Write *in*, *on*, or *under*. Draw lines.

1 The rats are ___**in**___ the desk.

2 The ducks are _____ the books.

3 The elephants are _____ the ruler.

4 The cats are _____ the desk.

5 The lizards are _____ the bag.

6 The spiders are _____ the pencil case.

## 3  Look and write.

1 __The spider is in the pencil case._____

2 _____

3 _____

4 _____

5 _____

# I like / I don't like . . .

**Language Focus**

Use **like** and **don't like** to express likes and dislikes.

☺ I **like** dogs.     ☺ I **like** dogs, too.

☹ I **don't like** dogs.

**1** Circle the correct words to complete the sentences.

1 I *like* / *don't like* dogs.

2 I *like* / *don't like* ducks.

3 I *like* / *don't like* cats.

4 I *like* / *don't like* frogs.

5 I *like* / *don't like* rats.

## 2  Complete the sentences with the words from the box.

> too   like   green   ~~like~~   don't   lizards

Ben   I **(1)** ___like___ dogs.

Tim   I like dogs, **(2)** _____ .

Ben   I **(3)** _____ like rats. What about you?

Tim   I like rats, and I **(4)** _____ lizards.

Ben   I like **(5)** _____, too. They are my favorite – big **(6)** _____ lizards!

## 3  Look and write.

1  I like cats. _____        2  _____

3  _____        4  _____

5  _____        6  _____

# Reading: A Project

**1** **Look at the pictures. Read the texts and choose *yes* or *no*.**

This is my cat. His name is Felix. He's nine. His favorite toy's his doll. Felix is a small brown and black cat. He's in my bag! I like cats. Cats are my favorite. I don't like dogs. What about you?

Sophie

This is my rat. Her name is Rita. She's five. Her favorite toy's her ball. Rita is a small white rat. I like rats. Rats are my favorite. I don't like cats. What about you?

Max

1 Felix is a rat.                                   *yes* / (*no*)

2 Felix's favorite toy is his doll.      *yes* / *no*

3 Felix is on the bag.                       *yes* / *no*

4 Rita is five.                                   *yes* / *no*

5 Her favorite toy is her doll.         *yes* / *no*

6 She is black and white.                *yes* / *no*

**1** **Write the sentences.**

**1** nine / is / years / old / Digby / .

_____

**2** is / white / He / .

_____

**3** ball / favorite / His / toy's / his / .

_____

**2** **Write about Digby. Use the sentences from Activity 1.**

# Listening: Animals

**1** 🎧 **07** **Listen and circle. Then draw the animals.**

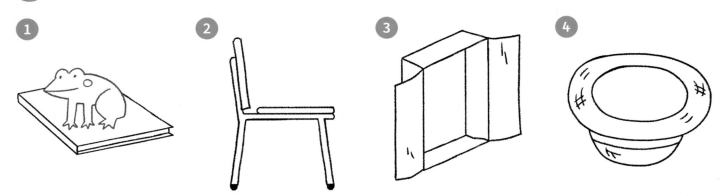

**1** The frog's (on) / *under* the notebook.   **3** The spider's *in* / *on* the box.

**2** The duck's *on* / *under* the chair.   **4** The cat's *in* / *under* the hat.

**2** 🎧 **08** **Listen and check ☑ or put an X ☒.**

| Animals | Jill | Bill |
|---|---|---|
| **1** | ✓ | ✗ |
| **2** | | |
| **3** | | |
| **4** | | |
| **5** | | |

**1** Find and circle six animals. Then play the memory game.

Where is the frog?

It's on the ball.

**2** Talk about the animals. Draw 😃 or 😞 for you and your friend.

I like elephants. What about you?

I don't like elephants.

😃 Me
😞 My friend

○ Me
○ My friend

○ Me
○ My friend

○ Me
○ My friend

**3** Work with your friend from Activity 2. Say.

Hi! I'm Tim. I like elephants and cats. Cats are my favorite! I don't like spiders, and I don't like lizards.

Hello! I'm Eva. I like …

# 4 I have / I don't have . . .

I have a cheese sandwich.

I don't have a cheese sandwich.

I have cake.

I don't have cake.

I have an apple.

Me too! I have a big green apple.

## Language Focus

Use **have** and **don't have** to talk about possessions.

I **have** a sandwich and an apple.

I **don't have** cake.

**1** **Look and write *yes* or *no*.**

1 I have cake. _____yes_____

2 I have bananas. _____

3 I have pizza. _____

4 I don't have peas. _____

5 I don't have chicken. _____

6 I have orange juice. _____

## 2 Complete the sentences with the words from the box.

Me   have   too   have   have   don't

1   I **have** a kiwi.   Me too!

2   I have pizza.   I _____ pizza. I have chicken.

3   I have cake.   Me _____!

4   What's for lunch?   I don't _____ chicken. I have sausages.

5   I have meatballs and peas.   I _____ meatballs, but I don't have peas. I have carrots.

6   I have a cheese sandwich.   _____ too!

## 3 Look and write.

1  I don't have cake.

2  _____

3  _____

4  _____

# Do ... have any ... ?

**Language Focus**

Use **Do ... have any ... ?** to ask about possessions.

Use **Yes, we do** and **No, we don't** to give short answers.

***Do* we *have* cheese?**      ***Yes, we do.***

                              ***No, we don't.***

---

**1** **Look at the pictures. Match the questions with the responses.**

1 Do we have any apples?

2 Do we have any bananas?

3 Do we have any orange juice?

4 Do we have any sausages?

5 Do we have any cheese?

6 Do we have any chicken?

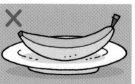

Yes, we do.      No, we don't.

## 2 Write the dialogue in the correct order.

Do you have sausage on your pizza?

Me too! I like sausages.

No, I don't. I don't like carrots. I have cheese.

Yes, I do. I have cheese and sausage. Sausage is my favorite.

Do you have carrots on your pizza?

Alice  Do you have carrots on your pizza?

Katy _____

Alice _____

Katy _____

Alice _____

## 3 Write questions.

1 Do we have any apples?      2 _____

3 _____      4 _____

5 _____      6 _____

# Reading: A Text Message

**1** Read. Check ☑ the food in the text messages.

sausages ☑     steak ☐     chicken ☐     pizza ☐

carrots ☐     peas ☐     bananas ☐     apples ☐

cheese ☐     apple juice ☐     orange juice ☐     milk ☐

**7.05 pm**

Hi, May! I'm at the store. I don't have my shopping list. Look in the kitchen and help me, please! Do we have any cheese?

Hi, Mom!
Yes, we do.

OK. Do we have any bananas and apples?

We have one banana.
We don't have any apples.

Do we have any chicken?

No. We don't have chicken, but we have eight sausages. We don't have pizza – pizza's my favorite!

OK, May! A cheese pizza, too!

**2** Look at Activity 1. Write the food words.

We don't have any **(1)** _apples_ . We have one **(2)** _____ ,
and we have **(3)** _____ . We don't have any **(4)** _____ or
**(5)** _____ , but we have eight **(6)** _____ .

**1** **Look and write the food.**

cheese

_____  _____

_____  _____

_____  _____

**2** **Look. Write a dialogue about the picture in Activity 1.**

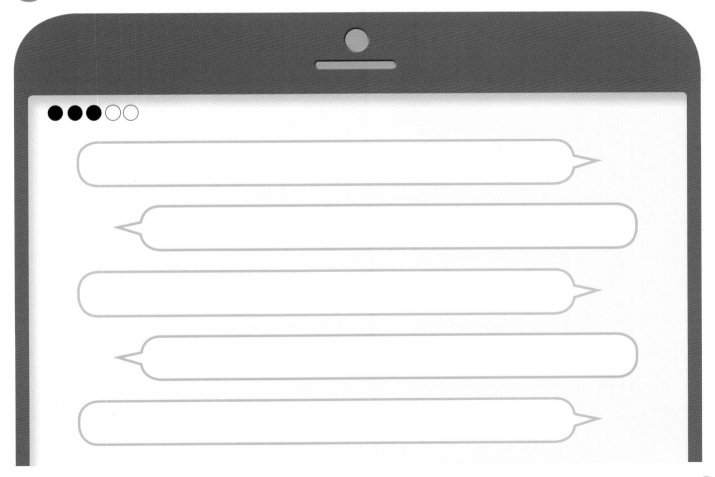

# Listening: Food

**1** 🎧 09 Listen and check ☑ Laura's birthday food.

**2** 🎧 10 Listen and match.

Leo and Rose    Mom and Nick    Ann and Jack    Dad and Tina

**1** What's in your fridge? Draw five things and say.

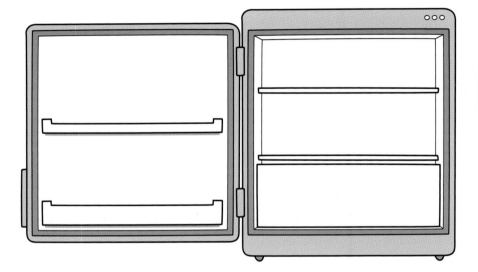

I have four carrots, six bananas, …

**2** Ask a friend about their fridge. Check ☑ or put an X ☒.

cheese ☐          fish ☐

apples ☐          peas ☐

pizza ☐           carrots ☐

sausages ☐        bananas ☐

chicken ☐         cake ☐

steak ☐

Do you have any cheese?

Yes, I do. Do you have any cheese?

No, I don't.

**3** With your friend, look at your fridges in Activity 1. Do you have the same things?

We have bananas and sausages.

# 5 Free-Time Activities

On Thursdays, I play soccer. What about you?

I go to school on Saturdays.

It's OK. School is cool.

I go swimming on Thursdays. I play soccer on Saturdays. What do you do on Saturdays?

On Saturday?!

**Language Focus**

Use the verbs **go ...** and **play ...** to talk about free-time activities.
*I **go swimming** on Mondays.*        *I **play soccer** on Saturdays.*

## 1 Match the sentences with the pictures.

1 On Mondays, I ride my bike. [d]

2 On Fridays, I play computer games. ☐

3 I go swimming on Thursdays. ☐

4 "What do you do on Sundays?"
  "I watch TV and sleep!" ☐

5 I play soccer with friends on Saturdays. ☐

6 On Tuesdays, I play with my toys. ☐

## 2 Circle the correct words to complete the sentences.

1 I *(play)* / *go* soccer on Saturdays.

2 I *play* / *go* swimming on Fridays.

3 What do you *do* / *go* on Thursdays?

4 I *ride* / *play* my horse on Sundays.

5 I *do* / *play* computer games on Tuesdays.

6 I *do* / *play* the piano on Wednesdays.

## 3 Write sentences with the words from the boxes and days.

> go   play   ride   watch

> ~~soccer~~   computer games   swimming   TV   ball   bike

1  I play soccer on Tuesdays.

2  _____

3  _____

4  _____

5  _____

6  _____

Tuesday

Monday

Saturday

Thursday

Friday

Sunday

# Do you . . . ? Yes, I do. / No, I don't.

Do you watch TV on the weekend?

Yes, I do.

No, I don't.

Do you play computer games on the weekend?

## Language Focus

Use **Do you . . . ?** to ask about activities. Use **Yes, I do** and **No, I don't** to give short answers.

***Do you watch*** *TV on the weekend?*
***No, I don't****.*

***Do you play*** *in the park on the weekend?*
***Yes, I do****.*

**1** **Write *Yes, I do* or *No, I don't*.**

1 Do you watch TV on the weekend?        ✗    <u>No, I don't.</u>

2 Do you play with your toys on Sundays?  ✓    _____

3 Do you play soccer on the weekend?      ✗    _____

4 Do you ride your bike on Tuesdays?      ✓    _____

5 Do you play in the park on the weekend? ✓    _____

6 Do you go swimming on Fridays?          ✗    _____

## 2 Match the sentences with the pictures.

1 Do you watch TV on the weekend?   [c]

Yes, I do.

2 Do you play computer games on Fridays?   □

Yes, I do.

3 Do you play computer games on the weekend?   □

No, I don't. I play soccer.

4 Do you watch TV on Sundays?   □

No, I don't. I read a book.

5 Do you play hide-and-seek on the weekend?   □

No, I don't. I sing with my friends.

6 Do you play soccer on Sundays?   □

Yes, I do.

## 3 Write the questions.

1 ride / Do / you / on the weekend / your / bike / ?

**Do you ride your bike on the weekend?**

2 Do / soccer / you / on Sundays / play / ?

_____

3 go / you / on the weekend / swimming / Do / ?

_____

4 you / hide-and-seek / play / on Saturdays / Do / ?

_____

5 watch / on the weekend / you / Do / TV / ?

_____

6 Do / the piano / play / you / on Mondays / ?

_____

# Reading: A Blog

**1** **Read the blog. Write Sam's schedule.**

## MyBlog

### Sam Brown

**My Week**

It's a busy week for me! On Monday, I play tennis for one hour, and on Tuesday, I swim for one hour. On Wednesday and Friday, I watch TV and read a book. On Thursday, I ride my bike with my friend Meg. We ride our bikes for two hours. Saturday is my favorite day! I go to the park and play with my friends. We play soccer. On Sunday, I watch TV and play computer games. What do you do on the weekend?

| Monday | Friday |
|---|---|
| play tennis | |
| Tuesday | Saturday |
| | |
| Wednesday | Sunday |
| | |
| Thursday | |
| | |

**1** **Write your schedule.**

| Monday | Friday |
|---|---|
| _____ | _____ |
| Tuesday | Saturday |
| _____ | _____ |
| Wednesday | Sunday |
| _____ | _____ |
| Thursday | |
| _____ | |

**2** **Write a blog. Use your schedule in Activity 1 to help you. Draw your picture.**

## MyBlog

# Listening: Free-Time Activities

**1** 🎧 **11** **Listen and draw lines.**

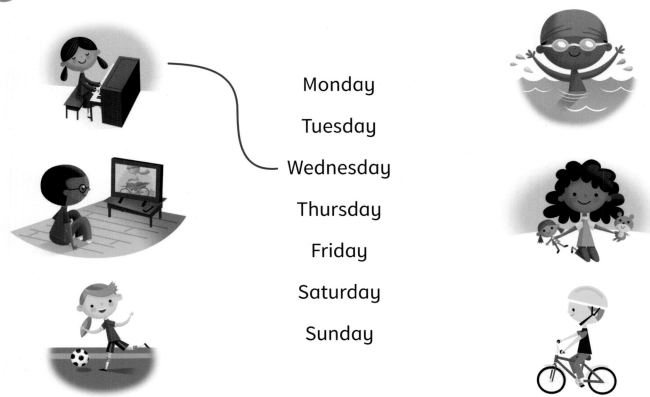

Monday

Tuesday

Wednesday

Thursday

Friday

Saturday

Sunday

**2** 🎧 **12** **Look at Jane's schedule. Listen and circle the correct activities.**

## Weekend Schedule

| Friday | go swimming
(play tennis) |
| --- | --- |
| Saturday | go swimming
play computer games
play board games |
| Sunday | play soccer
ride my bike |

**1** Look and do the actions.
Play the guessing game.

Number 3! You play computer games.

**2** Draw a picture of you on your favorite day.
Complete and practice.

My favorite day is _____ . I _____ and _____ on _____ .

**3** Talk about your favorite day.

My favorite day is Friday. I play soccer and ride my bike on Fridays.

# 6 There's / There are ...

There's a frog under the log.

Cool!

There are two beautiful butterflies on the flower.

Cool!

There's a big scary spider in the tree.

There's ... a monster under the table. Aagh! Oh, it's Spot!

## Language Focus

Use **there's** and **there are** to say what singular and plural nouns you can see.

**There's** *a monster.*     **There are** *four cats.*

**There's** *a frog.*           **There are** *three apples on the tree.*

## 1 Match the words with the pictures.

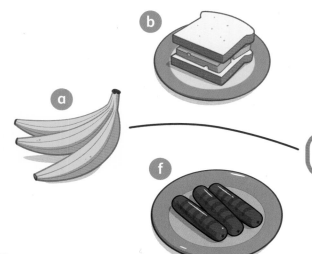

a

b

c

d

e

f

There's

There are

**2** **Write *There's* or *There are*.**

**1** __There's__ a cat in the living room.

**2** _____ five frogs in my bedroom.

**3** _____ a cat on the TV.

**4** _____ a frog in my bedroom.

**5** _____ a monster under the table.

**6** _____ two cats in the dining room.

**3** **Look and write.**

**1** There's a snake in the basement.

(a snake / basement)

**2** _____.

(a lizard / bedroom)

**3** _____.

(seven crocodiles / bathroom)

**4** _____.

(five tigers / yard)

**5** _____.

(a spider / kitchen)

**6** _____.

(a cat / living room)

**Language Focus**

Use **Is there … ?** to ask about singular nouns. Use **Are there … ?** to ask about plural nouns. Use **Yes, there is** and **No, there isn't** to give short answers about singular nouns. Use **Yes, there are** and **No, there aren't** to give short answers about plural nouns.

Use **How many … are there?** to ask about a plural number of things. Use **There are …** to give an answer about plural nouns.

| | |
|---|---|
| ***Is there** a plane?* | ***Yes, there is.*** |
| ***Are there** any rats?* | ***No, there aren't.*** |
| ***How many** cars **are there**?* | ***There are** four cars.* |

## ❶ Circle the correct words to complete the sentences.

1 **Are** / *Is* there any pears?

2 *Are* / *Is* there any rats?

3 How many cars *are* / *is* there?

4 *Are* / *Is* there a plane?

5 *Are* / *Is* there a go-kart?

6 How many cakes *are* / *is* there?

## 2 Look and write answers.

1 Is there a cat? **Yes, there is.**

2 Are there any balls? _____

3 Is there a frog? _____

4 How many sausages are there? _____

5 Is there a go-kart? _____

6 How many apples are there? _____

## 3 Look. Complete the questions and answers.

1 **Are there any** bikes? **Yes, there are.**

2 _____ cars? Yes, _____.

3 _____ are there? _____ eight kites.

4 _____ a plane? _____.

5 _____ a park? _____.

6 _____ are there? _____ one cake.

# Reading: A Project

**1** Read the text and the sentences. Write *yes* or *no*.

I live in a big house. It isn't old. It's new. There are four bedrooms, a kitchen, a dining room, a living room, and a hall. My bedroom is my favorite room. It's blue. There are posters of animals, and I have a green rug. There's a desk in my bedroom, and I have a computer. There isn't a TV. My toys are in my bedroom, and there's a teddy bear. I play with my toys on the weekend.

1 The house is small. ___no___

2 There are five bedrooms. _____

3 The rug is blue. _____

4 There isn't a computer. _____

5 There's a TV in the bedroom. _____

6 There are toys in the bedroom. _____

**1** Make notes about your house and bedroom.

Rooms                  My Bedroom                Adjectives

_____        _____           _____

_____        _____           _____

_____        _____           _____

**2** Draw and write about your house and your bedroom.

_____

_____

_____

_____

_____

_____

_____

_____

# Listening: Houses and Rooms

**1** 🎧 13 **Listen and number the rooms.**

**2** 🎧 14 **Listen to Amy. Circle the correct answers about her house.**

1 How many rooms are there?
  a There are seven rooms.
  **(b)** There are eight rooms.

2 How many bedrooms are there?
  a There are two bedrooms.
  b There are three bedrooms.

3 Is there a yard?
  a Yes, there is.
  b No, there isn't.

4 Is there a desk in the living room?
  a Yes, there is.
  b No, there isn't.

5 Are there any stairs?
  a Yes, there are.
  b No, there aren't.

**1** Find and circle six differences. Then say.

There's a yellow ball.

Bedroom A!

**2** Look at the bedrooms in Activity 1. Play the memory game.

How many pencils are there in Bedroom A?

There are …

Where is the teddy bear in Bedroom B?

It's …

What color's … ?

It's …

**3** Choose a bedroom from Activity 1. Talk about it.

This is Bedroom A. There's a yellow ball. It's on the chair. There are two red books. There are …

# 7 Do you like this/these . . . ?

Do you like these jeans?

Yes, I do!

Do you like these shoes?

No, I don't! Put on these shoes.

Do you like this jacket?

No, I don't! Put on this jacket.

Do you like this hat?

Yes, I do!

**Language Focus**

Use **Do you like this ... ?** to ask about singular nouns.
Use **Do you like these ... ?** to ask about plural nouns.
Use **Yes, I do** and **No, I don't** to give short answers.

*Do you like this hat?*       ***Yes, I do.***

*Do you like these shoes?*       ***No, I don't.***

**1** **Match the words with the pictures.**

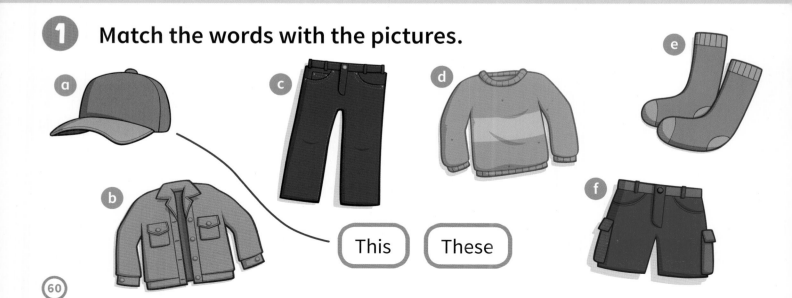

This    These

## 2 Write the questions.

1 this / Do / like / hat / you / ?  Do you like this hat?

2 these / you / shoes / Do / like / ? _____

3 like / jacket / you / this / Do / ? _____

4 like / you / shorts / these / Do / ? _____

5 T-shirt / Do / you / like / this / ? _____

6 you / jeans / like / Do / these / ? _____

## 3 Look and write.

1 Do you ___like this hat___ ?
☺ Yes, ___I do___ .

2 Do you _____ ?
☹ No, _____ .

3 Do you _____ ?
☹ No, _____ .

4 Do _____ ?
☺ _____ .

5 Do _____ ?
☹ _____ .

6 _____ ?
☺ _____ .

61

# Is he/she + -ing?

**Language Focus**

Use **Is he/she + -ing** to ask what people are doing. Use **Yes, he is** and **No, she isn't** to give short answers. Use **is + -ing** to describe what people are doing.

*Is he wearing* a blue T-shirt?          ***Yes, he is.***

*Is she wearing* brown shoes?          ***No, she isn't.***

*Olivia's wearing* a red sweater.

---

**1** **Look and read the questions. Write *yes* or *no*.**

1 Is Emma watching TV?  ___*yes*___

2 Is Paul playing a game?  _____

3 Is Lara singing?  _____

4 Is Ken playing a game?  _____

5 Is Emma wearing a green T-shirt?  _____

6 Is Ken wearing a blue sweater?  _____

## 7

**2**  **Write** *Yes, he/she is* **or** *No, he/she isn't.*

**1** Is he wearing
red shorts?
  **Yes, he is.**

**2** Is he watching TV?
  _____

**3** Is he wearing a
red sweater?
  _____

**4** Is she eating cake?
  _____

**5** Is he playing
soccer?
  _____

**6** Is she playing
computer games?
  _____

**3**  **Write the questions and sentences.**

**1** Anna / wearing / is / a blue skirt / .
  **Anna is wearing a blue skirt.**
  _____

**2** is / What / doing / Bob / ?
  _____

**3** Are / Amy and Hannah / bikes / riding / ?
  _____

**4** are / TV / watching / Emma and Tom / .
  _____

**5** playing / Oscar / soccer / is / .
  _____

**6** a sandwich / Kylie / Is / eating / ?
  _____

# Reading: A Chat

**1** **Read the conversation and answer the questions.**

| CHATS  School Friends | *James, Amy* |
|---|---|

**James Brown**

**Amy Little**

> Hi, Amy!

> I'm in my bedroom. I'm listening to music with my cat! He's on my bed!

>> Is he sleeping?

> Yes, he is.

>> Where are your mom and brother Luke?

> My mom's in the dining room, and Luke's in the living room.

>> Is your mom eating?

> No, she isn't. She's reading a book in her favorite chair!

**1** Who is James talking to?
He's talking to Amy.

**2** What is the cat doing?

**3** What is James doing?

**4** Where is Mom?

**5** Where is Luke?

**6** Is Mom watching TV?

## 1 Make notes.

You are at your house. What are you doing?

_____

What is your mom doing? Where is she?

_____

Do you have a cat or a dog? What is he/she doing?

_____

What is your brother/sister doing? Where is he/she?

_____

## 2 Write a conversation with your friend.

**CHATS** School Friends

_____

_____

_____

_____

_____

_____

_____

# Listening: Clothes

**1**  🎧 **15**  Listen and draw 😃 or ☹.

1  😊

2  ◯

3  ◯

4  ◯

5  ◯

6  ◯

**2**  🎧 **16**  Listen and match.

1 Stan    2 Oscar    3 Stella    4 Lucy    5 Maya

a    b    c    d    e

**1** **Play the description game. Use the words.**

> Bob

> Bob's wearing a yellow T-shirt and blue shorts. He's playing tennis.

**Helen**

> T-shirt
> shorts
> cap
> soccer

**Matt**

> sweater
> pants
> shoes
> TV

**Pat**

> jacket
> skirt
> banana

**Bob**

> T-shirt
> shorts
> tennis

**2** **Draw a picture of you wearing your favorite clothes.**
**Talk about your picture.**

> In this picture, I'm wearing my favorite clothes. I'm wearing …

**3** **Show your picture to a friend. Ask and answer.**

> Do you like this T-shirt?

> Yes, I do! Do you like these jeans?

# 8 Can/Can't for Ability

I can skip.

I can't skip.

I can touch my toes.

I can't touch my toes.

I can stand on one leg.

I can stand on one leg.

And I can stand on one leg, too!

**Language Focus**

Use **can** and **can't** to talk about ability.

*I **can** stand on one leg.*          *I **can't** touch my toes.*

*She **can** skip.*          *He **can't** skip.*

---

**1** Match the sentences with the pictures.

1 He can't swim.          **f**

2 He can play soccer.          ☐

3 He can skip.          ☐

4 She can stand on one leg.          ☐

5 She can't play the piano.          ☐

6 She can't ride a bike.          ☐

## 2 Write *can* or *can't*.

1

✗ He __can't__ swim.

2

✓ He _____ ride a horse.

3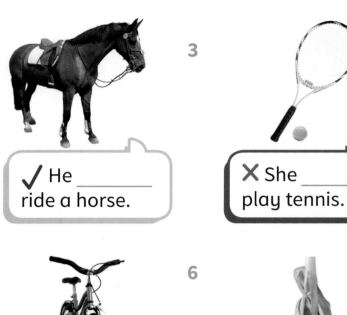

✗ She _____ play tennis.

4

✗ He _____ play the piano.

5

✓ She _____ ride a bike.

6

✓ She _____ do ballet.

## 3 Look and write.

|  | Ned | Alice |
|---|---|---|
|  | | |
| 🎹 | ✗ | ✓ |
| Hola | ✗ | ✓ |
| 🎸 | ✓ | ✗ |

1 __Ned can't play the piano.__

2 _____

3 _____

4 _____

5 _____

6 _____

# Questions with Can

**Can you play tennis?**

**Can you ride a horse?**

**Can you ride a bike?**

**Yes, I can!**

**No, I can't.**

**No, I can't.**

**Great! Let's go!**

## Language Focus

Use **can** to ask about ability. Use **Yes, I can** and **No, I can't** to give short answers.

*Can* you swim?　　　　**Yes, I can.**

*Can* you dance?　　　　**No, I can't.**

---

**1** **Match the questions with the responses.**

1 Can you dance?

2 Can you fly a kite?

3 Can you ride a horse?

4 Can you stand on one leg?

5 Can you play the guitar?

6 Can you swim?

a I don't know. Let's see. Whoa! No, I can't.

b Yes, I can. I can play the piano, too.

c Yes, I can, and I can sing.

d No, I can't. I don't have a kite.

e Yes, I can. I swim on the weekends.

f No, I can't, but I can ride a bike.

**2** **Complete the sentences with the words from the box.**

sing   speak   play   can   ~~Yes~~   can't

**Karl**  Hello, May. Can you dance?

**May**  (1) __Yes__ , I can.

**Karl**  Can you (2) _____ the guitar?

**May**  No, I (3) _____. But I can play the piano, and I can (4) _____.

**Karl**  Can you (5) _____ Spanish?

**May**  No, I can't. But my sister (6) _____.

**3** **Write questions.**

1 (play piano) __Can you play the piano?__

No, I can't. But I can play the guitar.

2 (speak Spanish) _____

Yes, I can. ¡Hola!

3 (play tennis) _____

No, I can't. I can play soccer.

4 (ride a bike) _____

Yes, I can. My bike is pink.

5 (swim) _____

Yes, I can.

6 (ride a horse) _____

No, I can't. I don't like horses.

# Reading: A Forum

**1** Read the text and the sentences. Write *yes* or *no*.

• • •

## Pet Forum

### Super Pets!

Alice

Can your cat sing?!

My cat is named Bob. He's black with one white foot! He's two years old. He can run and jump, AND he can sing! What can your pet do?

Harry

Wow! No way! My cat can't sing. I have a dog, too. His name is Patch. He can swim, and he can play soccer. We play soccer in the yard! Look at my photo.

Sally

Cool! I don't have a cat or a dog, but I have a horse. Her name is Jazzy. She's a big black horse. She's beautiful. She can't sing. She can jump up high and stand on two legs, and she can run.

1 Bob is one.      <u>**no**</u>

2 Bob can't sing.      _____

3 Patch can swim.      _____

4 Patch can't play soccer.      _____

5 Jazzy is ugly.      _____

6 Jazzy can run and jump.      _____

**1** **Choose a pet and make notes.**

Pet _____

What's her/his name? _____

What color is she/he? _____

How old is she/he? _____

She/he can _____

She/he can't _____

**2** **Write a forum post. Use your notes from Activity 1 to help you.**

Pet Forum

**Super Pets!**

_____
_____
_____
_____
_____
_____
_____
_____
_____

**1**   🎧 17   Listen and color.

**2**   🎧 18   What can Rita do? Listen and check ☑ or put an X ☒.

## What can Rita do?

talk ☑            jump ☐

walk ☐            dance ☐

run ☐             sing ☐

## 1 Ask and answer. Use the words from the box.

Can you touch your toes?

Yes, I can.

skip   make   fly   touch   swim   play   sing

## 2 Imagine and draw a robot. Complete and practice.

This is my robot. Her/His name's
_____. My robot can
_____, _____,
and _____. My robot can't
_____ or _____.

## 3 Talk about your robot.

This is my robot. His name's Rob. Rob can talk, sing, and jump. Rob can't dance or swim.

# 9 Suggestions

**Language Focus**

Use **Let's + verb** to make suggestions.

|  |  |
|---|---|
| | *Good idea.* |
| **Let's play** *the guitar.* | *I'm not sure.* |
| | *Sorry, I don't want to.* |

## 1 Match the sentences with the pictures.

1 Let's paint a picture. ☑ d

2 Let's take a photo. ☐

3 Let's look for shells. ☐

4 Let's listen to music. ☐

5 Let's go to the park. ☐

6 Let's go swimming. ☐

## 2 Complete the sentences with the words from the box.

~~Let's~~   idea   play   sure   eat   want

**Hugo** (1) _____Let's_____ look for shells.

**Tony** I'm not (2) _____.

**Hugo** OK. Let's (3) _____ soccer.

**Tony** Sorry, I don't (4) _____ to. We don't have a ball.

**Hugo** Let's (5) _____ ice cream.

**Tony** Good (6) _____. Banana is my favorite ice cream!

## 3 Look and write.

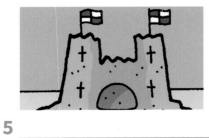

1 <u>Let's play the guitar.</u>
   ✓ ____Good idea.____

2 _____
   ✗ Sorry, _____.

3 _____
   ✓ _____

4 _____
   ✗ I'm _____.

5 _____
   ✗ I'm _____.

6 _____
   ✓ _____

# Where's / Where are ...?

**Language Focus**

Use **Where's ... ?** to ask about singular items.
Use **It's ...** to answer about singular items.

Use **Where are ... ?** to ask about plural items.
Use **They're ...** to answer about plural items.

| | |
|---|---|
| **Where's** the blue book? | **It's** in the green bag. |
| **Where are** the orange books? | **They're** in the black bag. |

**1**  Write the questions.

1  are / Where / small / the / shells / ?  **Where are the small shells?**

2  is / the / dog / Where / big / ? _____

3  are / blue / shoes / the / Where / ? _____

4  the / Where / is / cat / ? _____

5  beach / the / Where / is / ? _____

6  orange / Where / the / are / kites / ? _____

**2 Look and write answers.**

1 Where's the blue book?

It's in the green bag.

2 Where's the green lizard?

_____

3 Where are the green books?

_____

4 Where's the purple spider?

_____

5 Where are the red books?

_____

6 Where's the yellow lizard?

_____

**3 Look. Complete the questions and answers.**

1 Where 's the lizard ?

_____It's_____ in the bedroom.

2 _____ the crocodiles?

_____ in the bathroom.

3 _____ the cat?

_____ room.

4 _____ the spider?

_____

5 _____?

It's in the basement.

# Reading: A Magazine

**1** Read the text and answer the questions.

## Come to Wales

Wales is a beautiful country. There are lots of places to see. You can walk in the high mountains and swim in the ocean at the beautiful beaches. There are lots of mountains, but go to Snowdon Mountain. It's really high, so take your walking shoes! There are also lots of castles. Go to famous Conwy Castle. It's very old. You can walk to the top of the castle and take photos of the mountains and the ocean. You can see sheep, too! Have lunch in the Castle Café, and eat Welsh cakes! Wales is fantastic!

Welsh Cakes

Conwy Castle

**1** What adjectives can you find? What do they describe?

**beautiful country** _____ _____ _____ _____

**2** What activities can you do on vacation in Wales?

_____ _____ _____

**3** What is the name of the high mountain? _____

**4** What can you do at Conwy Castle?

_____

**5** What animals can you see from the castle? _____

**6** What food can you try? _____

## 1 Match the phrases.

1 walk up Ben Nevis    a bagpipe music

2 go to Edinburgh    b the Loch Ness Monster

3 listen to    c haggis (meat with onion)

4 eat    d a mountain

5 look for shells on    e a city

6 find    f the fantastic beaches

## 2 Write a magazine article about Scotland. Use the phrases in Activity 1 to help you.

# Listening: Vacations

**1**  🎧 **19**  Listen and check ☑ the correct picture.

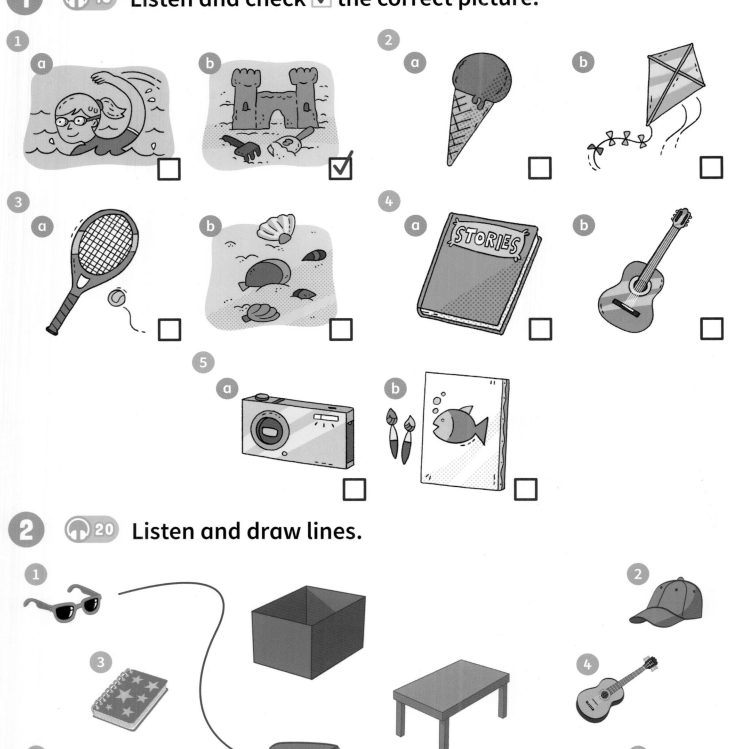

1
a  b ☑

2
a  b

3
a  b

4
a  b

5
a  b

**2**  🎧 **20**  Listen and draw lines.

1   2

3   4

5   6

# Speaking

**9**

**1** **You want to take these things on vacation. Where are they? Choose and circle.**

1 My T-shirts are *in my bag / on the table.*

2 My sunglasses are *on the table / on the chair.*

3 My guitar is *in the toy box / under the table.*

4 My books are *in my bag / on the table.*

5 My kite is *in the toy box / under the chair.*

6 My shorts are *on the chair / under the table.*

**2** **Ask your friend about the things in Activity 1. Check ✓.**

> Where are your T-shirts?

> They're on the table.

|  | 🎒 | 🪑(table) | 🪑(chair) | 📦 |
|---|---|---|---|---|
| 1 T-shirts |  |  |  |  |
| 2 sunglasses |  |  |  |  |
| 3 guitar |  |  |  |  |
| 4 books |  |  |  |  |
| 5 kite |  |  |  |  |
| 6 shorts |  |  |  |  |

**3** **With your friend, choose and color five activities for your vacation. Then say.**

> Let's catch a fish.

| catch a fish | take photos | read a book | paint pictures |

| make sandcastles | swim in the ocean | eat ice cream |

| look for shells | listen to music | play the guitar |

> I'm not sure. Let's look for shells.

> OK. Good idea!

# Audioscripts

## Welcome Unit page 10

🎧 01

**Sam:** Hello! I'm Sam. What's your name?
**Ana:** I'm Ana. How old are you, Sam?
**Sam:** I'm eight. How old are you, Ana?
**Ana:** I'm seven.

**Kim:** Hi!
**Dan:** Hello!
**Kim:** I'm Kim. What's your name?
**Dan:** I'm Dan.
**Kim:** What a nice name! How old are you, Dan?
**Dan:** I'm six. How old are you, Kim?
**Kim:** I'm nine.

🎧 02

**Sam:** I'm Sam. My hat is red.
**Ana:** I'm Ana. Look! My balloon is blue.
**Dan:** I'm Dan. My bag is green.
**Kim:** I'm Kim. Look! My balloon is orange.

## Unit 1 page 18

🎧 03

1 **Teacher:** What's this?
  **Girl:** It's a pencil case. It's green.
  **Teacher:** Yes, it's my pencil case!
2 **Boy:** Hmm. Is it a pen?
  **Girl:** No, it isn't. It's a pencil.
  **Boy:** OK. What color is it?
  **Girl:** It's blue.
3 **Girl:** What's this?
  **Boy:** It's a ruler.
  **Girl:** Yes, it is! It's your ruler!
4 **Boy:** Is it a book?
  **Teacher:** No, it isn't.
  **Boy:** Oh, it's a notebook!
  **Teacher:** Yes, it is.

5 **Girl:** What's this?
  **Teacher:** It's paper.
6 **Boy:** Look at my bag – it's purple.
  **Girl:** Wow! It's cool!

🎧 04

Open your pencil case, please. Now get a pencil. Look at this box, please. Now write your name on the box! And now … put away your pencil, please.

## Unit 2 page 26

🎧 05

1 **Boy:** What's this?
  **Girl:** It's my favorite toy. My doll.
  **Boy:** Oh, it's a beautiful doll!
  **Girl:** Thank you! Her name's Lulu.
2 **Girl:** How old are you?
  **Boy:** I'm seven.
  **Girl:** And how old is your friend Daniel?
  **Boy:** He's eight.
3 **Girl:** Look at this big blue monster!
  **Boy:** His name's Zak!
  **Girl:** Zak is ugly!
  **Boy:** Yes, but he's my favorite toy!
4 **Boy:** What's her name?
  **Girl:** Sara. She's my friend.
  **Boy:** How old is she?
  **Girl:** She's six.
  **Boy:** And what's her favorite toy?
  **Girl:** Her favorite toy's her new yellow kite.

🎧 06

Hi! My name's Oliver. My friend's name's Emma. She's seven. These are her favorite toys. Look! This is her big yellow ball. Yellow is Emma's favorite color. And this is her pink plane. It's new! And can you see the small green car? It's my favorite toy, too! Oh, no, it isn't … It's the long blue train!

## Unit 3 page 34

**1 Boy:** Oh, no! My frog isn't here.
  **Girl:** Look! Your frog's on your notebook!
**2 Girl:** My duck? It's not in the pond …
      Where is it?
  **Boy:** It's there! Look – under the chair.
**3 Ben:** Look, May – a spider!
  **May:** A spider? Where?
  **Ben:** On the box!
  **May:** *In* the box?
  **Ben:** No! *On* the box – there!
  **May:** Oh, yes! I can see it now.
**4 May:** Ben, where's the cat?
  **Ben:** The cat? Well, it's not under the tree …
      Oh, look – it's in the hat!
  **May:** The cat's in the hat!

### 08

**Jill:** Hey, Bill. Let's look at these pictures of animals. Look – a dog. I like dogs. What about you?

**Bill:** Hmm. I don't like dogs, Jill.

**Jill:** Oh, a lizard! I don't like lizards – they're ugly!

**Bill:** Ugly? Come on, Jill. Lizards are cool. I like lizards!

**Jill:** Oh, look at this donkey. I like donkeys. What about you, Bill?

**Bill:** I like donkeys too, Jill!

**Jill:** Hey, an elephant! I like elephants!

**Bill:** Me too! I like elephants – they're my favorite!

**Jill:** What's this, Bill?

**Bill:** It's a spider!

**Jill:** A spider? Oh, no! I don't like spiders!

**Bill:** I know. And I don't like spiders, Jill!

## Unit 4 page 42

Hello! I'm Laura, and it's my birthday! I'm seven today. Look – this is the food for my birthday. I have cheese sandwiches – they're my favorite! And I have sausages and … oh, yes! A pizza. I have a big pizza for my friends. I like apples, but I don't have apples today – I have bananas. Big yellow bananas. I don't have chicken, and I don't have carrots. Oh! But I have a beautiful cake – my birthday cake! Yummy!

### 10

**1 Leo:** I'm hungry, Rose. Do we have any cheese?
  **Rose:** No, we don't, Leo. We have peas!
  **Leo:** Peas? Oh, no! I don't like peas …
**2 Nick:** Mom, do we have any fish for lunch?
  **Mom:** Yes, Nick, we do. Here's the fish. You're hungry!
**3 Boy:** OK, Ann, do we have any cheese for the pizza?
  **Ann:** Let's see … Oh, no, we don't.
  **Boy:** Yes, we do. Look – this is cheese.
  **Ann:** Oh, yes! Yummy!
**4 Tina:** Mmm, Dad, is this for lunch?
  **Dad:** Yes, Tina. We have a big steak – your favorite!
  **Tina:** Yes, it is! Thanks, Dad.

## Unit 5 page 50

**Tess:** Hi! I'm Tess, and I play the piano. I play the piano on Wednesdays.

**Peter:** Hello! My name's Peter. I like TV! I watch TV on Saturdays. Saturday's my favorite day!

**Holly:** Hello! I'm Holly, and I play soccer. Soccer is great! I play soccer on Fridays.

**Jack:** Hi! I'm Jack. I like Mondays. I go swimming on Mondays!

**Anna:** Hi! My name's Anna. I play with my toys on Sundays. Yes, I play with my teddy bear and my doll on Sundays.

**James:** Hello! I'm James, and I like my bike. I ride my bike on … Thursdays … Oh, no! Not on Thursdays, on Tuesdays. That's right. I ride my bike on Tuesdays.

🎧 12

**Woman:** Hi, Jane! I have a question for you. What do you do on the weekend?

**Jane:** Well, I do lots of things!

**Woman:** Do you play tennis?

**Jane:** Yes, I do. I play tennis on Fridays.

**Woman:** Do you go swimming on Fridays, too?

**Jane:** No, I don't. I go swimming on Saturdays. And I play games with my family on Saturdays.

**Woman:** That's nice – do you play computer games?

**Jane:** No, board games.

**Woman:** Great! I like board games.

**Jane:** Me too! Oh, and on Sundays I ride my bike. I have a new bike!

**Woman:** Fantastic! And do you play soccer on Sundays, too?

**Jane:** No, I don't. I don't like soccer.

**Woman:** OK, that's all. Thanks, Jane!

## Unit 6 page 58

🎧 13

1 Look! There's a monster in the bedroom.
2 Now, the kitchen – there are two monsters. There are two monsters in the kitchen.
3 I can see a monster on the stairs. There's a monster on the stairs!
4 Look! There's a monster in the bathroom.
5 Can you see the hall? There are two monsters in the hall.
6 And now, the living room – there are two monsters in the living room.

🎧 14

**Mr. Smith:** OK, Amy. Tell us about your house. How many rooms are there?

**Amy:** Hmm. One, two … There are eight rooms. We have eight rooms, Mr. Smith.

**Mr. Smith:** Hmm! There are *seven* rooms in *my* house. And how many bedrooms are there?

**Amy:** There are three bedrooms. Three bedrooms and two bathrooms.

**Mr. Smith:** OK. And is there a yard?

**Amy:** No, there isn't. There isn't a yard, but there's a cool park near my house.

**Mr. Smith:** That's nice! Now, is there a desk in your bedroom?

**Amy:** No, there isn't. My bedroom's small. But there's a big desk in the living room. And it's for me!

**Mr. Smith:** Great! Now, the last question – are there any stairs in your house?

**Amy:** No, there aren't. My house is big, but there aren't any stairs.

**Mr. Smith:** OK! Thanks, Amy!

## Unit 7 page 66

🎧 15

1 **Boy:** Do you like these socks?
  **Girl:** Yes, I do.
  **Boy:** Me too!
2 **Girl:** Do you like this jacket?
  **Boy:** Yes, I like your jacket. You look good like that.
  **Girl:** Thanks!
3 **Boy:** Do you like these pants?
  **Girl:** Hmm … No, I don't. They're ugly.
4 **Girl:** Do you like these shoes?
  **Boy:** Hmm … No, I don't. I don't like the color.
5 **Boy:** Look at this sweater! Do you like it?
  **Girl:** Yes, I do. It's nice!
6 **Girl:** I like this T-shirt. What about you?
  **Boy:** Oh, yes, I like it, too!

🎧 16

**Eric:** Look, Dad! My friends are in the park!

**Dad:** Where, Eric?

**Eric:** There! Look, that's Stan. He's playing with the ball.

**Dad:** Oh! Is he wearing a red T-shirt?

**Eric:** Yes, he is. And look, that's Oscar! Oscar's wearing a blue baseball cap.

**Dad:** OK. I can see Oscar now. I like his cap!

**Eric:** Me too! Oh, and that's Stella – she's riding her bike.

**Dad:** Hmm. Is she wearing shorts?

**Eric:** Yes, she is. She's wearing orange shorts.

**Dad:** Oh, and is that Lucy?

**Eric:** No, Dad. That's Maya. Maya's wearing jeans, and Lucy's wearing a purple skirt.

**Dad:** Oh, I can see now. Lucy's wearing a purple skirt.

**Eric:** Yes, that's right!

## Unit 8 page 74

Hi! My name's Rita, and I'm a robot! This is my head – I have a big yellow head. And look! I have two hands – one and two. My hands are orange. Now, these are my arms. I have long arms! They're purple. I have purple toes, too! I have ten purple toes. And can you see these? They're my knees. I have two blue knees. I like blue!

**Ellie:** Look, Jack. This is my new robot, Rita.

**Jack:** Wow! She's cool! I like her long arms.

**Ellie:** Me too! She's great. She can talk! Listen.

**Robot:** Hi! My name's Rita.

**Jack:** That's nice. Can she walk, too?

**Ellie:** Yes, Rita can walk. Look!

**Jack:** Fantastic! Hey! Can Rita run?

**Ellie:** Uh … No, she can't. Rita can walk, but she can't run.

**Jack:** That's OK.

**Ellie:** Oh! But she can jump! Look at this.

**Jack:** Cool!

**Ellie:** And … she can dance! Look!

**Jack:** Hahaha, that's amazing! Hey! Can Rita dance *and* sing?

**Ellie:** Hmm … No, she can't sing … But you and I can! Come on!

**Jack:** All right, Ellie! You know I can't sing … But I can play with Rita!

## Unit 9 page 82

1 **Ben:** We're at the beach!

**Sara:** Hooray! Let's swim in the ocean!

**Ben:** Hmm … Sorry, I don't want to. Let's make a sandcastle.

**Sara:** OK. Good idea.

2 **Ben:** Sara! Let's fly the kites!

**Sara:** Oh, I don't have my kite. I'm hungry … Let's eat ice cream!

**Ben:** Mmm! Good idea!

3 **Sara:** Let's play tennis, Ben.

**Ben:** Tennis? At the beach? I'm not sure …

**Sara:** You're right! We can't play tennis here. Let's look for shells.

**Ben:** OK!

4 **Ben:** Sara, where's my book?

**Sara:** It's at home, Ben.

**Ben:** Oh … OK. Let's play the guitar, then.

**Sara:** Great idea! Here's the guitar.

5 **Sara:** Ben, look at this fish!

**Ben:** Wow! It's beautiful! Let's take a photo.

**Sara:** Good idea!

1 **Mary:** Mom, where are my sunglasses? They aren't on the table.

**Mom:** They're in your bag.

**Mary:** OK. Thanks, Mom!

2 **Mary:** Dad, where's my baseball cap?

**Dad:** Hmm … It isn't in your bag.

**Mary:** Oh, it's here. It's on the table.

3 **Mom:** Mary, your notebook isn't on the table. Where is it?

**Mary:** My notebook? It's in my bag, Mom.

**Mom:** OK, great.

4 **Dad:** Let's play the guitar. Oh, but … where's my guitar?

**Mom:** The guitar's on the table, Daniel.

**Dad:** OK, thanks, Sue!

5 **Mary:** My shoes aren't here … Where are they?

**Mom:** Look! They're in the box!

**Mary:** In the box? Oh, yes, they are!

6 **Mary:** Dad, are my cars on the table?

**Dad:** No, they aren't, Mary. Look – they're in the box.

**Mary:** Cool! Thanks, Dad.

# Acknowledgments

The authors and publishers acknowledge the following sources of copyright material and are grateful for the permissions granted. While every effort has been made, it has not always been possible to identify the sources of all the material used, or to trace all copyright holders. If any omissions are brought to our notice, we will be happy to include the appropriate acknowledgments on reprinting and in the next update to the digital edition, as applicable.

Key: U = Unit

## Photography

The following images are sourced from Getty Images.

**U1**: Lemon_tm/iStock/Getty Images Plus; jesadaphorn/iStock/Getty Images Plus; t_kimura/E+; urfinguss/iStock/Getty Images Plus; **U2**: Ismailciydem/ iStock/Getty Images Plus; **U3**: MmeEmil/E+; ozgurdonmaz/iStock/Getty Images Plus; Divesh_Mistry/iStock/Getty Images Plus; Smitt/iStock/Getty Images Plus; GlobalP/iStock/Getty Images Plus; 2happy/iStock/Getty Images Plus; photographer, loves art, lives in Kyoto/Moment; Arathrael Photography/ Moment; Ulianna /iStock/Getty Images plus; **U4**: Wavebreakmedia Ltd/ Wavebreak Media; Jose Luis Pelaez Inc/DigitalVision; Juanmonino/E+; vfoto/ iStock/Getty Images Plus; milanfoto/E+; gbh007/iStock/Getty Images Plus; etiennevoss/iStock/Getty Images Plus; **U5**: bowie15/iStock/Getty Images Plus; SDI Productions/E+; Fancy/Veer/Corbis; Asia Images/Photodisc; Big Cheese Photo; Icealien/iStock/Getty Images Plus; Tigatelu/iStock/Getty Images plus; **U7**: Issaurinko/iStock/Getty Images Plus; NYS444/iStock/Getty Images Plus; heinteh/iStock/Getty Images Plus; Olga Gillmeister/iStock/Getty Images Plus; Ng Sok Lian/EyeEm; mustafagull/iStock/Getty Images Plus; ValuaVitaly/iStock/ Getty Images Plus; somethingway/iStock/Getty Images Plus; KathyDewar/ iStock/Getty Images Plus; JudyKennamer/iStock/Getty Images Plus; Steve Prezant/Image Source; Compassionate Eye Foundation/DigitalVision; **U8**: Studio Light and Shade/iStock/Getty Images Plus; Creative Crop/Photodisc; viafilms/iStock/Getty Images Plus; popovaphoto/iStock/Getty Images Plus; Richard Coombs/EyeEm; ThePROmax/iStock/Getty Images Plus; JasonDoiy/ iStock/Getty Images Plus; scanrail/iStock/Getty Images Plus; Steve Prezant/ Image Source; Ami-Rian/iStock/Getty Images plus; kenex/DigitalVision Vectors; alexei_tm/iStock/Getty Images plus; **U9**: photoguns/iStock/Getty Images Plus; Firmafotografen/iStock/Getty Images Plus; tulcarion/E+; aedkais/iStock/Getty Images Plus; Joff Lee/Photolibrary; Mariusz Kluzniak/Moment Open.

The following images are sourced from other sources/libraries.

**U1**: spaxiax/Shutterstock; duckycards/iStockphoto; Tpopova/iStockphoto; oku/Shutterstock; Mosutatsu/iStockphoto; EuToch/iStockphoto; **U8**: tkemot/ Shutterstock; Alex White/Shutterstock; Cybernesco/iStockphoto; Riddy/ iStockphoto; carlosalvarez/iStockphoto; Mike Flippo/Shutterstock.

Commissioned photography by Stephen Bond.

## Illustrations

Anna Hancock (Beehive); Alan Rowe; Bernice Lum; Chris Lensch; Clive Goodyer; Daniel Limon; David Semple; Marek Jagucki.

## Audio

All the audio clips are sourced from Getty Images.

FRANCIS CERIONI/Sound Effects; Jupiter Images/Sound Effects; Sound Effects; Mirko Pernjakovic/Sound Effects; Michael Harrison/Sound Effects; Rok Stibler/ Sound Effects; Cedric Hommel/Sound Effects; LDj_Audio/Sound Effects.

Audio produced by Hart McLeod.